Asking for Help

Katie Peters

GRL Consultants,
Diane Craig and Monica Marx,
Certified Literacy Specialists

Lerner Publications ◆ Minneapolis

Note from a GRL Consultant
This Pull Ahead leveled book has been carefully designed for beginning readers. A team of guided reading literacy experts has reviewed and leveled the book to ensure readers pull ahead and experience success.

Lerner Publications Company
An imprint of Lerner Publishing Group, Inc.
241 First Avenue North
Minneapolis, MN 55401 USA

For reading levels and more information, look up this title at www.lernerbooks.com.

Main body text set in Memphis Pro 24/39
Typeface provided by Linotype.

Photo Acknowledgments
The images in this book are used with the permission of: © chengyuzheng/Getty Images, p. 3; © Lorado/Getty Images, pp. 14–15; © PeopleImages/Getty Images, pp. 8–9; © Prostock-Studio/ Getty Images, pp. 4–5, 16 (knife); © RyanJLane/Getty Images, pp. 6–7, 16 (milk); © Studio1One/ Getty Images, pp. 10–11; © yacobchuk/Getty Images, pp. 12–13, 16 (raincoat).

Front cover: © chee gin tan/Getty Images

Library of Congress Cataloging-in-Publication Data

Names: Peters, Katie, author.
Title: Asking for help / Katie Peters.
Description: Minneapolis : Lerner Publications, [2022] | Series: Helpful habits (pull ahead readers people smarts - nonfiction) | Includes index. | Audience: Ages 4–7 | Audience: Grades K–1 | Summary: "Show young readers where and when to ask for help: when something is too heavy or sharp, while in a pool, or while crossing a street. Pairs with the fiction title Help, Please!"— Provided by publisher.
Identifiers: LCCN 2020015583 | ISBN 9781728403502 (library binding) | ISBN 9781728423180 (paperback) | ISBN 9781728418346 (ebook)
Subjects: LCSH: Help-seeking-behavior—Juvenile literature.
Classification: LCC HM1141 .P48 2021 | DDC 158.3—dc23

LC record available at https://lccn.loc.gov/2020015583

Manufactured in the United States of America
1 - 48346 - 48888 - 1/22/2021

Table of Contents

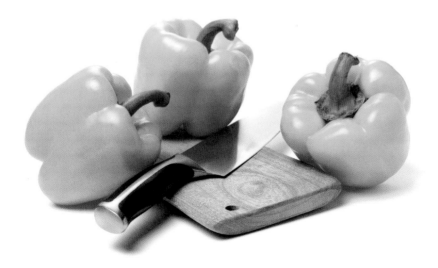

Asking for Help

The knife is sharp.
I ask Dad for help.

The milk is heavy.
I ask Mom for help.

The shelf is high.

I ask Dad for help.

The water is deep.

I ask Mom for help.

The zipper is stuck.
I ask Dad for help.

The road is busy.

I ask Mom for help.

Can you think of a time when you asked for help?

Did You See It?

knife

milk

raincoat

Index